Henceforth I Ask Not Good Fortune

poems by

Dotty LeMieux

Finishing Line Press
Georgetown, Kentucky

Henceforth I Ask Not Good Fortune

Copyright © 2020 by Dotty LeMieux
ISBN 978-1-64662-379-2 First Edition
All rights reserved under International and Pan-American Copyright Conventions. No part of this book may be reproduced in any manner whatsoever without written permission from the publisher, except in the case of brief quotations embodied in critical articles and reviews.

ACKNOWLEDGMENTS

Much gratitude to the literary outlets who first published the pieces listed below:

Woman Her World on Skids: Gyroscope, 2019; *Marin Poetry Center Anthology*, 2019

Solstice: *Writers Resist*, issue #88, February, 2019

An earlier version of Mayday: "Let Us Not Blame Foolish Women," 1983, Tombouctou Books

For a Poet I Once Loved and Stealing the Souls of Strangers: July, 2019, *Poetica Review*

The Dress: "Purifying Wind," 2020, Moonshadow Sanctuary Press

A big thank you to Donald Guravich for his wonderful cover art here and on past books

Thanks also to Thomas Centolella and the poets of the College of Marin Master Poetry workshop

The title of this collection, "Henceforth I Ask Not Good Fortune," is from Walt Whitman's transformative poem Song of the Open Road, from the 1856 edition of Leaves of Grass—the place I always go when I get stuck.

Publisher: Leah Maines
Editor: Christen Kincaid
Cover Art: Donald Guravich, copyright © 2020
Author Photo: Stephanie Mohan, Creative Portraiture
Cover Design: Elizabeth Maines McCleavy

Order online: www.finishinglinepress.com
also available on amazon.com

Author inquiries and mail orders:
Finishing Line Press
P. O. Box 1626
Georgetown, Kentucky 40324
U. S. A.

Table of Contents

Woman Her World on Skids 1

Solstice 3

Unaccompanied Minors 5

America Sends More Thoughts and Prayers 6

Mayday 8

For a Poet I Once Loved 9

The Toothbrushes are Kissing 10

Just to let you know 11

Ah Death 12

Salt Hospital 1 13

Mortality Hospital 2 15

Overheard at San Rafael Joe's Haibun 1 16

Stealing the Souls of Strangers Haibun 2 18

The Dress Haibun 3 20

Skip to My Lou My Darling 23

"Henceforth I ask not good-fortune, I myself am good-fortune"
—Walt Whitman, Song of the Open Road

Woman her World on Skids

Paused at the red light, I see her—
Urban traveler at a crossroads,
waiting out the light
weighted by her world on skids behind her
Arms bent back holding the plastic
reins of flattened cardboard
bearing the world—
not aloft as Atlas—
but on folded boxes that can be opened
into shelter,
black plastic bags, the heavy kind
for cramming every bit of trash
you clear from your property
before you move in or everything
you call your own
as you move out

In her bags she has crammed husband
House, children now grown, job
in a bank or a store
or a factory in another state

Nice clothes or rags
an apartment, tenement, old folks' home
crazy house
the faraway lap of ocean
on foreign shore
wing of white bird soaring

I watch her adjust the weight, knuckling
gnarled hands into locked grip
Bearing the more private, the more precious, cargo
on her bent back not a bit
of slack in sinewy limbs, face taut as a fist, eyes
tight against unforgiving sun, not an ounce of wanting
to be here but with steadiness
because after all, she is moving

if not quite upright, at least, not quite
prone, and with purpose

As the light changes.

Solstice

It's delivery day at St. Vincent's Dining Room.
men unloading trucks with bread, canned goods, day-old
everything for the homeless
and the not-yet homeless
hanging on by the skin of their teeth,
the ones who have teeth
and the ones who only have the skin

Scruffy off-white hair,
long brown coat like a cape
swirling around bony shoulders,
gap toothed smile, a man
picks bagels one, two, three
from a giant plastic bag open on the sidewalk

The sidewalk not crowded yet,
the bagel bag still fairly full,
the man in the brown cape-like garment
has his pick, takes his time choosing
plain, seeded, onion,
maybe a spicy cinnamon one
to summon the spirit of the Season

Face lit up with his choices, clutched
in his two hands as he starts across the street,
hair blowing around his face,
cape billowing out behind his slender frame,
he is transformed into a Romantic poet,

reciting odes
in a proper British accent,
to adoring listeners
gathered in the glittering firelight
of the local pub,
his hands gesturing freely,
accentuating the high points
of his lyricism

Back on B St., he strides in front of my car,
stopped now to let him pass, to watch
his coat-tails fly in his wake,
like autumn's last leaves
swooshing around us, into the street, launched
by winter's first insistent breath

Unaccompanied Minors
>*Caravan—"a company of travelers on a journey through desert or hostile regions"* Merriam-Webster dictionary

Caravans of migrants, he warned, are advancing on the border
Coming to test our defenses, breach our fortifications
coming to rape and pillage bringing gangs and drugs and children
an infestation

Stopped at the red light at Hetherton and 3rd
I see children, dark skinned, caravans
without wheels on the streets of San Rafael
Twenty, fifty, 100 children in neat rows
Unaccompanied minors in Gap tees, plaid shirts
high tops and pink leggings
Arms around each other laughing
The occasional red head or blond girl with pert pony tail
jostling the brown boys pairs of eyes shining: blue, green, brown

Coming in waves attacking the intersections
The light pulsing 5, 4, 3, 2, 1 walk!

Here there are no mothers weeping, their children torn from their arms,
no fathers bent like old men under the burden of everything they own

Here the light changes in quiet order, timed to section their line
Neatly, they obey as I move forward; the children keep coming
Aliens; the taste of dust in their mouths
Legs raw from scaling walls; seeking asylum in the high school
shelter on the soccer field; happiness in a Gringa's embrace
Children of no land

But here they are on a sunny spring afternoon
in San Rafael California
owning the sidewalk following all laws respecting all borders

Unaccompanied minors waiting out the light, polite and watchful
Never tempting fate or the cars that hurtle past them ignorant
angry or just plain unseeing.

America Sends More Thoughts and Prayers

Another shooting, another chance
for thoughts and prayers, America

Let me help you direct them:

>   Send thoughts to poverty and injustice
>   inequality and crazy on every
>   street corner
>
>   Send them to felony stars and porn stars
>   to jails overflowing
>   to shelters cold and unwelcoming
>   to storefront churches,
>   needles, vomit and human
>   waste
>
>   And don't forget the children
>   of Hiroshima
>   and Nagasaki
>   of Mi Li
>   and Aleppo
>
>   of Flint Michigan
>   and Parkland Florida
>   Charlottesville Virginia,
>   Orlando Florida
>   and Christchurch New Zealand

Send your prayers here America:

>   Pray to the immigrant
>   homeless, the drunkard
>   to the lady in pink who sings alone
>   in the park, surrounded by pigeons

The veteran in his chair
beside the shuttered window
or the one on the median who
only wants a smile and a wave

Pray to the sea otter,
the caged tiger in the zoo
who has forgotten his homeland
the tiny buds of spring struggling
to break the crust
of winter

Pray to the founding fathers
and the Iroquois nation
the babies you misplaced
and the fathers looking for them

 to Leticia who cleans my house
Victoria who hides in the doorway
and all the nameless ones
from shithole countries

America, this you can do:

    We know you'll never be able
    to make amends—
    But at least get down
    on your knobby knees,
    hang your hoary head,

              and cry

Mayday

You stand in the doorway looking out and I walk
along the front of the bar to where you wait
    Hi Comrade—I say. *Let's shake hands and*
    make up, shall we?

You take my hand and look straight into and through
    my eyes as though there were some truth
    between us, some unspoken knowledge
    that everything would be all right in the end

    I hope you don't think—you say, *that there are any*
    hard feelings on my part

It is not yet dusk outside the bar; it is the workingman's hour
Time for a game of pool
    a couple of beers
    a line of coke in the women's bathroom
    before dinner

Your gaze is straight—*I've been working so hard*—you say
I understand I'm not to take it personally and turn to go
    back to my seat

Later, on my way to the door, I look up to see you sitting
    on the closed-down pizza counter, eyes blank as the underside
    of a frying pan

You give me the thumbs up gesture as I go out
    into the now-dusky night
    where I drop my sweater into a puddle
    as the skies clear after the last rain of the season

For a Poet I Once Loved
> *"Immature poets imitate; mature poets steal."* T.S. Eliot;
> *The Sacred Wood: Essays on Poetry and Criticism, 1920*

Sorry that I took your words
for mine; but I did leave
your silk purse with the rainy day
fund; and I refrained from drinking the new wine
you were saving for inspiration

and the coveted red cowboy boots which were tempting
and so much more practical than ruby slippers

I could have taken those abstractions of yours
that pay the rent
and keep the lights on
and the gas flowing

the common household necessities
that fuel the body and the mind
and keep the *blah blah blah* dripping
    from your oh-so-ripe-for-the-plucking
    tongue.

The Toothbrushes Are Kissing

On the ledge under the bathroom mirror, like they are passing each other in the hall, like two lovers working different shifts, one coming the other going, clocks set by different alarms, by night and by day, by car and by bus; they meet on the landing careful not to wake the children, get the dog riled up. *What's the weather how's the traffic see you at breakfast?*

They pass and draw one to the other, bristles stiffening, reaching out and whisking by, barely touching—an air kiss like they might be French then back again like they might be magnets they never let go until torn apart by rough human hands—one from one. Molecules move between them spreading DNA.

Human hosts scrub scrub scrub the night away exchanging grunts shake and rinse clean enough replace in separate holders backs turned.

Lights out.

Just to let you know
With apologies to William Carlos Williams

I polished off
the prunes in
the cupboard
which you were probably
planning to eat
for regularity
Sorry, I needed them
more; I was hungry and
the chip bag was empty
If it's any comfort
they were dry and only
gave me gas

Ah Death
> *"It's after the fourth of July and we're all having a wonderful time and thinking about death"* Mary Tilson, KPFA, July 9, 2017

Death, cut it out.

Can't you give it rest, hang up your reaper's robes for a while; you're a workaholic; don't you know that's not healthy; stop being so damned persistent; you are a pest; you are not my friend, did you think you were? Does anyone love you even sloppy suicides; even depressed writers obsessed with their own hoary mortality?

Death, I'm on to you. You take us by degree; first you send age, then you start in on the bones, now the mind is in your sights; you trickster, you thief, you cartoonist's delight (but not mine); you surprise and hang around like the unwelcome guest everyone feels sorry for, but can't wait to get rid of.

I do not feel the least bit sorry for you, any more than the deer feels sorry for the car, the foot feels sorry for the root, the exploding head pities the gun; I don't like you one bit, in fact, you suck, you are not wanted, now kindly go away you creep, you stalker, you molester of innocence; get back in your hell, visit your devil brother; sing *him* your dirges; rattle *his* bones; tell *him* your dead man tales.

Death, time to take a load off; you look like shit; you should rest; you might like it; you might feel at peace at last; stop being such a control freak and let us sort it out ourselves; don't worry, we'll join you when we're ready; really you don't have to do anything but wait; we'll come to you, believe it.

Ah Death, at least get down under the desk and beg like a dog.

Salt Hospital 1

Cocooned
in a room of my own
but nothing like what Virginia Woolf imagined
The furnishings for one thing
Narrow bed with rails, plain white sheets
Machine behind my head to check my vital signs
every few hours
I'm still alive, waiting out my sentence
Something has interrupted my sodium
All those years being told to drink more water
Watch your salt intake
Now it's the opposite
in this bland world
of whites and beiges
but all the salt I want

In ancient times salt was used
as currency
precious
like incense and myrrh
But not quite worth its weight in gold
Preservative for fish and even mummified human remains
A valuable commodity
to be traded
and hoarded
and fought over

Once, ocean
covered all
then sea creatures and finally
land creatures crawled to shore,
carrying ocean in their veins. Human
blood contains the same percent of salt
as the ocean, flowing through tributaries
of veins to every outpost of the body

When I take the dogs to the beach I say *–No!*
Don't drink the ocean
You'll puke

Here it's a salt cocktail
Three times a day
Potato chips
French fries

If you spill salt, they say,
toss a pinch of it over your left shoulder
to blind the Devil
and ward off the bad luck he's just itching
to bring you
Mine comes in square tablets dissolved
in a cup of microwaved water
No muss, no fuss, nothing to spill

Two days of tests and salty liquids, then
home with a prescription
for three salt pills a day
and admonitions not to drink too much
water, coffee, wine, it's all the same
when you're trying
not to pee
out all the salt
you just swallowed

and end up
like some old forgotten steer,
dried to sun-bleached bones
straining to reach the last salt lick
on the plains.

Mortality Hospital 2

In the room next to mine, a woman's voice calls for *Mom!*
Then *Brian!*
Then just yells *Hello!* over and over
until her vocal chords give out altogether
When I pass by her room on one of the walks
prescribed to stave off pneumonia,
she's sitting in a chair near the open door,
silent and frizzed like an out of focus photograph
of herself

I try to be sympathetic; she's old
She has no one
She doesn't know where she is or what's happening
To her in this strange place
But I mostly hope she doesn't continue
Wailing into the night

When Ray comes to visit, the nurse hands us both
advanced health care directives to read and fill out
for when we can no longer express ourselves coherently
like the woman next door crying out
for phantoms who never come
Do we want to be resuscitated, kept on life support?
Tubes that snake out of our arms
into beeping machines at our sides?
Only if there's chance—says Ray
For a decent quality of life
I don't want to be a vegetable, or unable to move or talk

Soon the woman next door begins calling out again—*Brian*
Brian! Then—*Hello Hello!*—growing increasingly hoarse,
Or that—says Ray, gesturing to the wall next to the visitor chair,
Pull the plug if I get like that

I don't tell him she has no plug to pull
And no one to pull it, even she did.

Overheard in San Rafael Joe's   Haibun 1

I meet my husband for dinner in San Rafael Joe's. At the next table a thin-faced gray haired man whose light colored eyes flash between a deep grey and an angry sea foam blue depending on the intensity of his speech, is talking in low but easily overheard tones, to a woman of about the same age, which appears to be about the same age as me, that is the late sixties, or in the era they are discussing, the early twenties.

Since the woman has her back to us, leaning toward him, her shoulders stooped, her gray head bobbing from time to time, I can only hear his part of the conversation. He is bent almost double over the table, as he speaks—*They flunked me because I didn't go to classes. I got a B on the final, and I said to the teacher, 'Can't you just give me a D minus?' I mean, I got a good grade on the test.' Didn't he care that he was sending me off to Vietnam? Now, I was 1A and would be drafted.*

> men heading off to war
> never enough room for bodies
> bent and bowed in battle

I said to him, 'you're sending me off to Vietnam to get killed, don't you care? Give me a D minus; I did well on the final. That must count for something.'

He didn't care, can you believe it? He said, 'You didn't come to classes. So you don't get to pass.'

So I say, 'But I did well on the test. I got a B, even though I didn't go to class. You're making me 1A and sending me to get killed in Vietnam.'

He didn't care. 'You have to come to class. It's a requirement. I don't care if you got an A plus on the final. If you don't attend the classes, you fail.'

That was cold. I tried to join the National Guard, but I got drafted. Right away. This was before the lottery; once you were 1A, they got you. Just like that. No time to get over the shock. That one professor could have kept me from going, if he'd just given me a D minus."

        bearing scars of youth
        old men keep silent
        tell only internal tales

I still can't hear what the woman is saying, though I am listening very hard. My husband is eating leg of lamb and I am eating a chicken pesto salad. I can't see what food is on the plates of the man and woman at the next table, but it doesn't look as if they've eaten much of it. The man pauses what amounts to a monologue now and then to sip his beer. The woman just nods and murmurs. Is she is wife, his girlfriend, someone he just met on line? I'll never know.

I want to reach out to the man; I want to reach across the years to when he was a student with an unforgiving teacher and I was advising young men to—just say no. I want to stand up at the table and tell him he doesn't have to go even if he flunks out of school. Even if he was drafted. He could refuse. But, I lack a time machine, and we finish our meal and leave the restaurant before I find out if he ever actually got to Vietnam.

This man, so abiding, so exposed, he might have been a ghost.

        clouds bunch and gather
        settling into winter
        smells of advancing storm

Stealing the Souls of Strangers Haibun 2

We are strangers in this diner, 1971 Alabama, a group of Northern journalists on vacation. With my borrowed camera, I have been charged to "document the trip." But maybe those words were not to be taken seriously? The South is a timeless place of fog and moss and molasses rivers, bathrooms in filling stations reading *white* and *colored*. The journalists try to fit in, smile sweetly, politely praise the canned cherry pie, accept more coffee. Everyone in this place is white, it goes without saying, even us.

The waitress' name is Crystal, embroidered on her cap. She holds a bottomless pot of coffee. Men she knows, big rig men, ranch hands, hangers on, call out—*Hey Crystal*—or—*Hey hon!* or just grunt and incline their heads toward their empty cups.

> time ticks or is stopped
> eyes turned within gaze without,
> feign obedience

I'm not sure you should—starts one of the journalists, as I click, shoot the dark haired man at the counter under the sign reading "Grade A Everything." And click, at Crystal, who doesn't notice or doesn't care or doesn't want to antagonize. And click, at the other man I think looks like Woody Guthrie if Woody Guthrie was still alive and out of work, and out of luck. The journalists worry, but no one shows anger or pleasure or even surprise.

> alligators with eyes closed
> look like logs, submerged, still,
> waiting

We leave, not hurrying, as we pile back into the red van. The journalists will take notes tonight in their tent, camped someplace safe, if such a place exists. If not—and how can you possibly know?—they will find a motel or drive through the night to New Orleans, where the streets are crowded and no one is from there. My film waits, safely tucked in its black box, until we reach the Berkeley darkroom where I will unspool and release the souls of all the strangers locked inside.

>   birds like small airplanes
> lift from the murk, ascend toward branches
> of trees that are not there

The Dress   Haibun 3

1.
1949

She stands, one slim-fingered hand on hip, the other reaching inside the open rear window of a hump-backed car, the kind you see only in old pictures of your parents; her right hand on her hip, cocked at a flirtatious angle, posing to please unseen photographer; smiling, preening, teasing. The man, we assume it is a man, crouches low to improve the line of sight, captures classic Athenian bone structure— Grecian nose, head held high, hair back raven black against milky sky.

My mother (I wish I knew her then!) proud, poised in new blue dress accenting slenderness of waist, hips that mold to delicate splayed fingers; hips that have probably been caressed a thousand times by the man who now caresses her entirety of face, hair, body, eyes, catching her soul in his lens, the way primitive people's souls are caught and held and sometimes enslaved by the camera's unforgiving eye.

And let me tell you about that dress! It fits her like the skin of a newborn colt, like the feathers of a hummingbird in flight, like smooth bark of a eucalyptus tree before molting; she and dress melding as one, the thicket of hair a mystery framing a face that exists as an extension of that magnificent dress.

No one else could ever wear such a dress.

A dress of that blue they call navy; a field of flowers in yellow and white (I imagine—the picture is in black and white) splashed across the night of her supple body; navy as the Navy blues my father wears to sweep her off her dainty feet into this car, this life, this picture; Providence Rhode Island 1949, picture I sweep into the album with all the others taken from that time until the end of childhood.

> from her bower of scented pine
> the blue bird chants the wonder
> of first newly cracked egg

2.
1971

This is the day I follow a woman, compelled, stalking her along a Manhattan street, my camera angled downward, synchronizing my steps to hers, snapping as I go, her bag slapping at her side, Capezio shopping bag adorned with Modigliani face familiar as the face of the woman by the car —dark hair swept back, eyes older, unsmiling, lips pursed like a woman who knows more than she bargained for— thwacking at the women's thigh, against the dress she wears, Navy blue, sprinkled with yellow and white flowers, vintage rayon dress circa 1949 (I imagine) smart once more New York City 1971.

I do not know this yet; how can I? I am a visitor here, with my borrowed camera brought with me to steal the souls of strangers, as they call to me that way only strangers can. All I know is propulsion forward, that face now stylized on a plastic bag, holding dancing slippers, a tiger patterned leotard, or maybe only her lunch. I am drawn by the face on the bag and not the woman carrying the bag. If I look up at her; if I see the cant of her head, her hair might be blonde; she might be impossibly tall or fat; something tells me not to look, and my camera carries itself and me back to the face moving ahead and down and then finally out of range of my prying lens.

And that dress, fabric slick and worn and loved and smooth and loose and swaying about the knees, dazzling in sunlight, capturing me as I capture it; sealed away inside my mysterious black box and saved like a treasure, like a bird's nest fallen from an apple tree in the last strong wind of winter. Like a talisman I do not know the meaning of

> posing, I throw back my head
> to reflection, miming laughter,
> still unable to crack open and soar

3.
2015

Today, unpacking the past, digging through layers of unremembered memorabilia, I find, then frame, the two photos, forgotten until this move, hopefully the last. Placing them side by side, I stand stunned before twins; faces long, one laughing, the other not, one alive, the other cartoonish, a caricature of the first; but the dress! It arrests my brain, overwhelms the prints, collapses the years between, flower for flower, swirl for swirl, fabric for fabric. This dress, oh, yes, maybe mass manufactured in rayon after silk went extinct during the war, and fabric was scarce and saved, and passed down, and dresses went to thrift stores for fashion-retro minded 70's chic chicks until today it reaches its final destination, in black and white on my wall, chemically preserved the way a corpse is drained of all color and saved for later reincarnation and remembrance.

> in the park buzzards
> one two three take flight and wheel
> into thin air

Skip to My Lou, My Darling

1.
Skipping, you are bound to trip on the hitch
in the sidewalk where the tree roots push it up
and land splat on your face, glasses
flying

2.
The way your heart skips a beat
when you spy your true love across the barroom
but can't get there in time to stop another from leading him
into dance

3.
When we were young, Lisa and I skipped out
on the check at Chez Panisse's upstairs café
We didn't mean to but the bill never came
and the door was open

4
The girl with coltish legs crossing the parking lot
her arms like sticks, and tall as a young oak
How many meals did she skip to have that
disappearing look?

5.
How long until she vanishes altogether, her mother hoping
her schoolmates just skip the funeral
no one could prevent, no amount of square dance tunes
karaoke or prom invitations could cajole her out of?

Dotty has been writing since the fifth grade when, at the urging of a literary minded teacher, she created an illustrated and bound version of her short story called "Arnold and the Dragon" about a hero dragon who put out fires (instead of starting them) and saved the home of the young human who befriended him.

She is the author of three previous chapbooks: *Five Angels*, Five Trees Press, 1976; *Let Us Not Blame Foolish Women*, Tombouctou Press, 1983; *The Land*, Smithereens Press, 1988. In the late 1970's through the mid-1980's she edited the literary magazine *Turkey Buzzard Review*, in collaboration with writers, artists and assorted talented helpers in Bolinas California.

Dotty studied at the New College of California Poetics Program and with poets Joanne Kyger, Edith Jenkins and Thomas Centolella. After taking time away from poetry to attend law school and become involved in Democratic politics, she picked it up again in the last few years.

She still works as an environmental attorney and campaign consultant and is proud to have been a Bernie Sanders delegate to the 2016 Convention. She lives and writes in Marin County California with her patient husband and two dogs.

She has recently started keeping a writing blog, where more work can be found: *https://www.dottylemieuxpoemsandmore.com/*

www.ingramcontent.com/pod-product-compliance
Lightning Source LLC
LaVergne TN
LVHW041519070426
835507LV00012B/1681